LIES

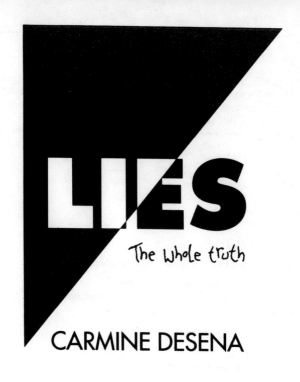

LIES

The Whole Truth

CARMINE DESENA

A PERIGEE BOOK

The author and publisher wish to acknowledge *The Utne Reader* for its inspiration and contribution to ''Lies of Our Times,'' which appear throughout this book.

Perigee Books
are published by
The Putnam Publishing Group
200 Madison Avenue
New York, NY 10016

Book design: H. Roberts

Library of Congress Cataloging-in-Publication Data

DeSena, Carmine.
    Lies: the whole truth/Carmine DeSena.
       p.   cm.
    ISBN 0-399-51820-7 (acid-free paper)
    1. American wit and humor. 2. Truthfulness and falsehood—Humor.
    I. Title.
    PN6231.T74D47   1993   93-3241   CIP
    818'.5407—dc20

Printed in the United States of America
1   2   3   4   5   6   7   8   9   10

This book is printed on acid-free paper.

CONTENTS

"The best way to make a long story short is to tell the truth."

PAUL HARLAN COLLINS

INTRODUCTION

Lying means not ever having to say you're sorry.

In compiling this book I was shocked to discover how much we human beings lie and to whom. James Patterson and Peter Kim, authors of *The Day America Told the Truth,* write that "lying has become a cultural trait in America. Lying is embedded in our national character. Americans lie about everything—and usually for no good reason." But the high priestess of morality, Sissela Bok, claims that our reasons for lying are innumerable. In *Lying: Moral Choice in Public and Private Life* she writes that we lie to: coerce, avoid, be tactful, make people feel better, prevent perceived harm, get what we want, get people to like us, appear reasonable, justify, deceive, avoid blame, have power, support the best interests of others, keep appearances and, of course, for national security.

So the next time someone says "Would I lie to you?", they probably already have. But then again, chances are you lied to them first.

LIES
WE
TELL
OURSELVES

"Mendacity is a system that we live in.
Liquor is one way out an' death's the other."

Tennessee Williams, *Cat on a Hot Tin Roof*

Lies of Our Times

DELUSIONS

▲ I'm 21.
▲ I'm a lousy liar.
▲ I read *Playboy* for the interviews.
▲ Things have never been better.
▲ I could have any man/woman in this room.
▲ I'm 39.

Lies of Our Times

I'M NOT FAT . . .

- ▲ I'm big-boned.
- ▲ I retain water.
- ▲ It's in my genes.
- ▲ It's not fat, it's cellulite.
- ▲ I have a very low metabolism.
- ▲ It's not fat, it's muscle.
- ▲ I have a thyroid condition.
- ▲ I weigh the same as I did in college.

THE "DO I LIE TO MYSELF?" QUIZ

How better to test your affinity for lying than assessing if you lie to yourself. How many of these statements have you made?

Please answer true or false (what else!) to the following:

1. I'll start my diet tomorrow.
2. I haven't changed but everyone else looks so much older.
3. I could quit smoking in a minute but I enjoy it too much.
4. Sex isn't everything.
5. So I'll be a little late, who'll notice?
6. There were no calories in that.
7. Everybody else does it.
8. I didn't want to go to that party even if I was invited.
9. Who wants to get married anyway?
10. I'm sure they didn't mean to forget my birthday.

THE "DO I LIE TO MYSELF?" QUIZ SCORECARD

For each question you answered **true,** give yourself a point.

No points: Not only do you lie to yourself, but now you're lying to a book. Doesn't that concern you?

1–3 points: You have begun the journey into the land of self-deception.

4–6 points: You are passing the point of no return.

7–9 points: You feel your parents rejected you—with good reason.

10 points: Call Doctor Kevorkian: you have no reason to live.

Lies of Our Times

I WANTED TO BLOW YOU OFF BUT INSTEAD I SAID:

▲ We couldn't find a baby-sitter.
▲ Oh, too bad, I'm busy that night.
▲ I lost your phone number.
▲ I must have been in the shower when you called.
▲ "We're not able to come to the phone at this time."
▲ We got lost.
▲ I missed the bus.
▲ The phone stopped just as I got to it.

LIES
WE
TELL
OTHERS

"Young as he was, his instinct told him that the best liar is he who makes the smallest amount of lying go the longest way."

Samuel Butler, *The Way of All Flesh*

THE "I NEVER LIE TO OTHERS" QUIZ

You hate when people lie to you, but how upset are you when you lie? Answer true for any of the following you've uttered:

1. I only had one.
2. I haven't taken so much as a pen home from the office.
3. I'm sorry I didn't say hello. I didn't see you.
4. I couldn't eat another bite.
5. It wasn't *that* expensive.
6. I gave at the office.
7. I really needed this.
8. I didn't know it was yours.
9. I've never betrayed a confidence.
10. Of course this is my natural color.

THE "I NEVER LIE TO OTHERS" QUIZ SCORECARD

For each **true** response, give yourself a point.

No points: Who are you—Mother Teresa? And if you are, why are you reading this book?

1–3 points: You're a pretty honest person or, since you figured out the scoring from the last quiz, you're lying.

4–6 points: You're the type that goes to church and "forgets" the donation envelope at home.

7–9 points: You probably married for money and steal from your friends after sleeping with their spouses.

10 points: You're either a lawyer or a politician.

Lies of Our Times

IT'S NOT MY FAULT, REALLY!

▲ I don't remember anything about it.
▲ I'm normally not like this.
▲ I was only doing 55.
▲ I only had two.
▲ I think I accidentally threw it away.
▲ My alarm didn't go off.

IT'S A FACT

Sixty-four percent of Americans confess that they would lie when it suits them, so long as it doesn't cause any real damage.

From The Day America Told the Truth

Lies of Our Times

LOOKING A GIFT HORSE IN THE MOUTH

▲ I love it.
▲ It's perfect.
▲ I've never seen anything quite like it.
▲ How did you know?
▲ I have one already.
▲ I'm sure I'll find a way to use it.
▲ It's just what I wanted.
▲ I've been thinking about buying this for myself.
▲ It is unique.
▲ The color is beautiful. What would you call it?

Lies of Our Times

LIES OF KINDNESS

▲ I love your new suit.
▲ You look wonderful. Have you lost weight?
▲ You haven't changed a bit.
▲ No, of course I don't think your nose is too big. I love a strong profile.
▲ Grandma, you'll live to be 100.
▲ Don't be silly, it's back in style.
▲ You made it from scratch. I could never tell.
▲ Tuna Artichoke Surprise. Sounds yummy.

Sixteen percent of the men and eight percent of the women surveyed believed it was all right to tell a lie to get even with someone.

From The Day America Told the Truth

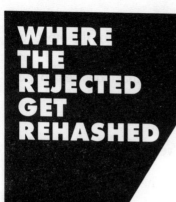

WHERE THE REJECTED GET REHASHED

"A lie with a purpose is one of the worst kind, and the most profitable."

Finley Peter Dunne

Most retailers know that every return has its story. But it's not usually a true one. Here's their list of the most common, if not particularly creative, fabrications . . . and, according to our sources, the truth that hides behind them.

▲ It's not my size. (I don't like it.)

▲ It's not sized properly. (I've gained weight.)

▲ This brand runs large. (My chest is too small.)

▲ This brand runs small. (My hips are too big.)

▲ The size was marked wrong. (I'm a larger size but don't want to admit it.)

▲ It's stained. (I was showing it to a friend at lunch and I spilled coffee on it.)

▲ It looks like it was worn! (I wore it to a party but it's too expensive to keep.)

▲ It's ripped! (. . . when I was pulling the tags off!)

▲ It looked like a different color in the store. (I forgot my glasses at home when I went shopping.)

▲ I have one already. (I'm such a shop-a-holic I don't remember what I bought yesterday.)

▲ It doesn't go with anything I own. (It doesn't go with anything period.)

▲ I found it cheaper. (I couldn't afford it in the first place.)

▲ It doesn't do anything for me. (I was depressed when I bought it but I feel better now.)

▲ My husband didn't like it. (It's too expensive.)

▲ My wife didn't like it. (She says it's embarrassing.)

▲ I can't wear it to work. (I just lost my job and really can't afford it now.)

▲ It makes me look fat. (I am fat but I won't admit it to myself or a store clerk.)

▲ It makes me look matronly. (The last thing I want is to look my age.)

▲ I got it as a gift and I already have one. (I hate it!)

TRUTH IS STRANGER
THAN LIES

▲ I bought it for my aunt. She died.
▲ I decided that I had to put my life in order and this
  was in the way.
▲ My mother-in-law sent me this. I hate her.
▲ My husband threatened to divorce me if I kept it.
▲ I bought it for my son but he outgrew it overnight.

WHAT PEOPLE LIE ABOUT MOST

▲ Their weight.
▲ How much money they make.
▲ Their hair color.
▲ How much junk food they eat.
▲ Their age.
▲ The college they went to.
▲ How drunk they got.
▲ The amount of exercise they do.
▲ How much something costs.
▲ How hard they work.
▲ How well their children are doing.

THE CONSEQUENCES OF TRUTH

''And after all, what is a lie but the truth in masquerade.''

LORD BYRON

''A truth that's told with bad intent beats all the lies you can invent.''

WILLIAM BLAKE

''Truth is stranger than fiction to some people but I am reasonably familiar with it.''

MARK TWAIN

"There is nothing as powerful as truth and often nothing as strange."

DANIEL WEBSTER

"Men occasionally stumble over the truth, but most of them pick themselves up and hurry off as if nothing happened."

SIR WINSTON CHURCHILL

"In this world, truth can wait; she's used to it."

DOUGLAS JERROLD

"Truth, sir, is a cow, which will yield skeptics no more milk; so they have gone to milk the bull."

SAMUEL JOHNSON

"Often the surest way to convey misinformation is to tell the strict truth."

MARK TWAIN

"The most awful thing that one can do is tell the truth. It's all right in my case because I'm not taken seriously."

GEORGE BERNARD SHAW

"If one tells the truth, one is sure, sooner or later, to be found out."

OSCAR WILDE

"It is hard to believe that a man is telling the truth when you know that you would lie if you were in his place."

H. L. MENCKEN

"If you want to be known as a liar, always tell the truth."

LOGAN P. SMITH

Lie and the world lies with you; tell the truth and the world lies about you.

You can't win: if you tell lies people will distrust you; if you tell the truth people will dislike you.

Truth is what's left over when you run out of lies.

"The pure and simple truth is rarely pure and never simple."

OSCAR WILDE

Beware the half truth: you may have gotten the wrong half.

As long as the truth is naked, men will continue to take liberties with her.

Money talks, but it doesn't always tell the truth.

LOVING
AND
LYING

"In human relationships kindness and lies are worth a thousand truths."

Graham Greene

LIES MEN TELL WOMEN

▲ We can still be friends.
▲ You're like a sister to me.
▲ I'll call you tomorrow.
▲ My wife doesn't understand me.
▲ I'm going to leave my wife.
▲ Of course I'll respect you in the morning.
▲ I never met anyone like you.
▲ I'm a one-woman man.
▲ No, I would never think of cheating.
▲ I don't care what it costs.
▲ Of course I remembered your birthday.
▲ I love foreplay.
▲ I'm working late.
▲ I've never said this to anyone before.
▲ I've got a headache.

LIES WOMEN TELL MEN

▲ I have to wash my hair.
▲ I'm on the Pill.
▲ Foreplay isn't that important.
▲ My husband isn't sensitive to my needs.
▲ I'm leaving my husband.
▲ You're the first one I felt anything for.
▲ Sorry, I'm having my period.
▲ It doesn't matter how much money you have.
▲ It's okay, it happens to everyone.
▲ Size isn't important.
▲ I never thought it could be like that.
▲ I'm not interested in marriage.
▲ I love football.
▲ I've got a headache.

"Some men were born to lie, and women to believe them."

JOHN GAY

"A man who won't lie to a woman has very little consideration for her feelings."

OLIN MILLER

"The charm of marriage is that it makes a life of deception absolutely necessary for both parties."

OSCAR WILDE

All men are liars, but some are not found until after they are married.

"A man finds it awfully hard to lie to the woman he loves—the first time."

HELEN ROWLAND

"Women have a hard enough time in this world: telling
them the truth would be too cruel."

H. L. MENCKEN

Some women find it hard to tell a lie; others can tell it
as soon as their husbands open their mouths.

It's not considered lying if you lie only when
complimenting a woman.

"One can always recognize women who trust their
husbands; they look so thoroughly unhappy."

OSCAR WILDE

"With a man a lie is the last resort; with women
it's first aid."

GELETT BURGESS

READING BETWEEN THE LIES

THE PERSONAL AD

he drinks

early fifties

19-year-old bimbo

not his real teeth

Fred seeks Ginger. Straight, white, male nonsmoker, mid forties, seeks young-at-heart woman. I've been called handsome and have a movie-star smile. I wish to explore new horizons with an understanding woman. I enjoy dancing and curling up in front of a fireplace. If you enjoy the same send a photograph and background info to Box B42 Grand Central Station, New York, New York 10023.

by his mother

someone he can manipulate and impress easily

he wants to be spanked

especially in topless clubs

too cheap to take her out

or if you can just read this ad

where he is actually living

a financial statement

Lies of Our Times

THE BLIND DATE

▲ You look exactly like your description.
▲ I never do this either.
▲ We certainly have a lot of things in common.
▲ I love Indian food.
▲ I date several times a week.
▲ You're an accountant. How interesting.
▲ It's true. "Attractive" can mean many different things.

Much of the lying done by men should be blamed on women: they insist on asking questions.

▲ Do I look fat?
▲ Are you seeing anyone else?
▲ Will you call me?
▲ Can you fix this?
▲ Are you staring at that woman?

FAMILY
FIBS

"Sacred family! . . . The supposed home of all virtues where innocent children are tortured into their first falsehoods . . ."

August Strindberg

Lies of Our Times

FAMILY FIBS

▲ Stay as long as you want.
▲ No, of course I don't mind lending you a little something to tide you over.
▲ You mean you can't stay for dinner? I'm so disappointed.
▲ What are families for?
▲ We never mind watching your child (dog or plants).
▲ Mom, I'm dying to talk to you too, but I was just going out.
▲ Uncle Steven, you're my favorite too.
▲ We love seeing you.
▲ I would love for Mom to come live with us. . . .

Lies of Our Times

LIES TO TELL A NEW MOTHER

▲ You've lost all the extra weight.
▲ The baby is adorable.
▲ The baby looks just like you.
▲ The baby looks just like its father.
▲ That's a lovely name. Does it mean something?
▲ They'll grow out of that.
▲ It's a phase. Eventually the whole head forms.
▲ They're such a pleasure at this age.
▲ Before you know it, the baby will sleep through the night.
▲ Only 12 hours in delivery. You were lucky.

Lies of Our Times

SIBLING RIVALRY

▲ Mom liked you best.
▲ Mom liked me best.
▲ I wish we were closer.
▲ If you need money, just call.
▲ Funny you should call, I was just thinking about you.
▲ No, I don't mind having everyone for the holidays.
▲ You're adopted.

Lies of Our Times

LYING-IN-LAW

▲ Of course I know you're only trying to be helpful.
▲ No, I welcome your opinion.
▲ I didn't say you were wrong. I said you were incorrect.
▲ I'd love for you to teach me to cook that the way you do.
▲ You're just like my own parents.
▲ It wouldn't be a holiday without you.
▲ I'd love to call you Mom.
▲ I know you hate to interfere.

LIES HUSBANDS TELL WIVES

▲ I'm happy your mother is coming.
▲ I was out with the boys.
▲ I hate that you have to work.
▲ Perfume smell, oh, I was looking for a present for you.
▲ I'm working late.
▲ I'm not angry.

LIES WIVES
TELL HUSBANDS

▲ It was on sale.
▲ I learned how to do that in *Cosmopolitan*.
▲ I don't mind, really.
▲ I was at the beauty parlor.
▲ A toaster, it's wonderful.
▲ I don't care about material things.

IT'S A FACT

Eighty-six percent of Americans confess to having regularly lied to their parents.

From The Day America Told the Truth

TELL ME A STORY: WHEN KIDS LIE

"Pretty much all the honest truth telling in the world is done by children."

Oliver Wendell Holmes

Like adults, children lie for attention, to avoid chores, out of fear, to control, for approval, but most important, because their parents teach them to.

That's right, parents teach their children to lie. The most deeply entrenched fibs ironically involve religious holidays: the annual pilgrimages of Santa Claus, the Easter Bunny or Elijah are among the most enduring; or, for some unknown reason, dental work—in the form of the Tooth Fairy. Many lies are a campaign of terror and intimidation: the bogeyman or the sandman. These never tricked any child into obeying or sleeping, but they are a first-class introduction to fear and manipulation. And our condoning lies is confirmed when you force your child to tell Aunt Zelda that you're not home when she calls. Teaching your child to lie is like not getting your car fixed. Sooner or later it will backfire on you.

KIDDIE CONCOCTIONS

If you're a parent who suspects your child is a prodigy of prevarication, you're likely to find many of the following scenarios all too familiar. And, if you're at your wits' end without a witty response, a few suggestions are provided.

All the other kids are going.
I know. That's why you're not. I want you to be an individual.

Those are not my dirty magazines
(drugs, cigarettes, etc.).
Well, then we'd better call the police. Someone is breaking into your room and leaving things.

I didn't break curfew. In California it's only 9:00 P.M.
That's true. So I'll only ground you until it snows in Los Angeles.

I don't know how it broke.
That's too bad. I'll have to punish you for a lack of evidence.

I'm not experimenting with drugs (sex or alcohol).
That's true. It appears the test trials are over and you're a full-fledged success.

I lost the change from the store.
That's a shame, because it was your allowance.

Of course I'm a virgin.
So am I.

MOTHER GOOSE AND OTHER PARENTAL TALES

Not wanting to show favoritism, it's only fair to provide children with answers to the most common lies parents tell.

When I was in school I was a straight A student.
Yeah, but there was less to learn back then.

If you do that, you'll go blind.
Great! Then I can get the dog you never let me have before.

When I was your age we didn't have food like this.
So why do we have to eat it now?

I found you in a cabbage patch.
What exactly were you doing there?

If you don't stop making that face, it will stick that way.
Don't you want me to be a chip off the old block?

This is going to hurt me more than you.
Couldn't we change it then, so it hurts me more than you?

I'm doing this for your own good.
I realize that, but I wish you thought less of me.

Your father and I waited until we were married.
Looking at you both, I can see why.

IT'S A FACT

Fifty-six percent of men and 35 percent of women believe that it is all right to lie in order to keep one's job.

From The Day America Told the Truth

RÉSUMÉS, REPORTS AND OTHER FICTIONS IN THE WORK-PLACE

"Occasionally, words must serve to veil the facts. But this must happen in such a way that no one becomes aware of it; or, if it should be noticed, excuses must be at hand, to be produced immediately."

Niccolo Machiavelli

"Everybody lies to me: the job applicants, the employers, even my own staff," complained a placement counselor. Whether head-hunting executive positions or supplying file clerks in hard times, the lies go up as the economy goes down.

"I can't start my job today. My grandmother's house blew up and I have to help her move."

"I can't go to work today. My uncle's dead on the floor."

"Of course I'm a professional proofreader. I read my roommate's papers in school for years."

"Yes, I can use a Dictaphone. What exactly is it?"

"Oh, I've been using that computer system for years. Could you just turn it on for me?"

"I can type 60 words a minute easy, except on a test."

FROM THE OFFICE OF HUMAN RESOURCES

"One woman told me she went to Yale. She did, in fact—for her cousin's graduation."

When a woman was asked about the degrees she listed on her résumé, she replied that she hadn't lied. She had included them as her educational *goals*.

"Another applicant said that she did so well they gave her a BSA."

"One man said he had two years' experience in financial credit processing. Later we found that meant he was a bank teller making deposits."

"One agency sent over a secretary with impeccable references that they said had been verified. She was pleasant but couldn't read."

"An employment agency touted another executive assistant as being worldly and able to speak six languages. Too bad one wasn't English."

Lies of Our Times

LIES THEY TELL JOB APPLICANTS

▲ Everyone else who has applied has better qualifications.
▲ The salary is negotiable.
▲ It's strictly a nine-to-five job.
▲ The benefits are excellent.
▲ Most of our employees have been with us forever.
▲ Vacation requests are flexible.
▲ We have an attractive retirement package.
▲ We're even thinking about profit sharing.

Lies of Our Times

LIES JOB APPLICANTS TELL

▲ I'm very well liked at my present job.
▲ My family has never interfered with my job.
▲ If I have to work weekends, it's not a problem.
▲ I'm very proud of my organizational skills.
▲ I want to be part of a team.
▲ The salary is less than what I'm making.
▲ I've had so many jobs because I've been looking for the right situation. I think this is it.
▲ I can be bonded. Definitely!
▲ I resigned.

Lies of Our Times

LIES BOSSES TELL WORKERS

▲ Your pension fund is safe.
▲ I want you to work independently.
▲ I hate for you to miss lunch.
▲ I empathize with the fact that you have a family.
▲ My last secretary was twice as fast.
▲ Our firm has no plans to relocate.
▲ We're just one big happy family here.

Lies of Our Times

LIES WORKERS TELL BOSSES

▲ I really enjoy working for you.
▲ No, this is not a personal call.
▲ I did it yesterday. It must have been misplaced.
▲ No, I don't mind doing it over.
▲ I worked through lunch.
▲ I'm feeling sick; I won't be in.

IT'S A FACT

Lying to your boss or co-workers is the #2 office crime. (It ranks just slightly below stealing office supplies and equipment.)

From The Day America Told the Truth

PROFESSIONAL CONFESSIONAL

"The devil is the father of lies, but he neglected to patent the idea, and the business now suffers from the competition."

Josh Billings

IT'S A FACT

In a nationwide survey, Americans ranked the professions for honesty and integrity. The following rated a "C" or below: lawyer, real estate agent, insurance salesman, rock and roll star, congressman, street peddler, prostitute, TV evangelist, organized crime boss, drug dealer.

From The Day America Told the Truth

Lies of Our Times

THIS WON'T HURT A BIT AND OTHER MEDICAL MENDACITIES

▲ This should only take a second.

▲ I may be able to save that tooth.

▲ It's not an infection, it's an inflammation.

▲ I'm sorry to keep you waiting.

▲ This fluoride treatment will taste just like mint.

▲ I've done this procedure hundreds of times.

▲ Believe me, the alternative was worse.

Lies of Our Times

"THE DEVIL MADE ME DO IT" AND LESSER LIES FROM THE CRIMINAL CLASS

▲ I didn't do it.
▲ I've never been in trouble before.
▲ I was buying those drugs for a friend.
▲ I was just trying it on.
▲ Hey, I was just looking for a customer-service person.
▲ I was at home with my mother.
▲ It must have fallen into my bag.

Lies of Our Times

STOCK-AND-BULL STORIES

▲ Don't worry, your account is sound as a rock.
▲ When I invest your money, I feel like it's my own.
▲ The market's never been more secure.
▲ Your money is safe with me.
▲ I bought the same stock for my mother.

READING BETWEEN THE LIES

OPEN HOUSE

stucco walls, orange shag carpeting, flocked wallpaper

all peeling

reputed site of 18th-century mass murder

no central heating

2 closet-size cubbyholes and a paneled windowless room in the basement

sits in the room

or are these bedrooms?

smoke trap; now houses a family of squirrels

it faces the highway

Historical colonial features original painted woodwork and other fine period details; master bedroom for a cozy couple with en suite tub plus three bedrooms make this a perfect family home. Spacious closets, eat-in kitchen and fireplace, situated on a private wooded lot, this dream house is located near major transportation, schools and shopping. Desperate owners have already relocated, so you can move in tomorrow.

it has been abused by three generations of toddlers, teenagers and their pets

if you don't mind standing and holding your food

where teen street gangs hang out all night and terrorize the neighborhood

hunters use the property for target practice all season long

once the squatters have been evicted

they're serving 10-20 for running a crack house

there's a 7-Eleven on the corner where kids cop pot

Lies of Our Times

FIFTY FABULOUS ACRES IN FLORIDA

▲ This building is so solid that you won't even know you have neighbors.
▲ The market is hot, hot, hot.
▲ Wait if you want, but I have a couple from New Jersey who are very interested.
▲ It's priced way below market.
▲ There's no asbestos in this building.
▲ You don't see this kind of home on the market every day.

Lies of Our Times

CLERICAL QUIBBLERS AND OTHER MISINFORMATION SYSTEMS

▲ The fax machine is out of paper.
▲ My computer is down.
▲ Someone must have misfiled it.
▲ You never gave it to me.
▲ She's on the other line and there's one call holding already.
▲ He's in a meeting.
▲ Your call will be answered in the order it is received.
▲ For more information, press 1.
▲ The check is in the mail.

Lies of Our Times

"THERE'S A SUCKER BORN EVERY MINUTE."

P. T. BARNUM

▲ It was owned by a little old lady who only drove it on Sundays.
▲ One size fits all.
▲ It looks wonderful on you.
▲ This offer will not be repeated.

IT'S A FACT

As further confirmation of our distrust of authority, 32 percent of Americans think they've been lied to by a clergyman. The same applies to accountants (34 percent). And in the case of lawyers, people say it in spades: Forty-two percent believe that they've been lied to by attorneys.

From The Day America Told the Truth

EXTRA! EXTRA!

"Once a newspaper touches a story, the facts are lost forever, even to the protagonists."

Norman Mailer

Tabloids: they're the underbelly of the news world. They thrive on innuendo, pain and scandal. And how we all love to linger at the supermarket checkout for our bit of titillation. But in your weekly forays, have you honed your detection skills to separate the truth from the lies? Here are 25 headlines, most of which were found in the pages of today's papers—but not all. Can you tell the real headlines from the fabrications? How far can the truth be stretched?

1. Girl 7, Pregnant for the Second Time
2. Woman Brings Husband Back from Dead to Kill Him Again
3. Living Elvis Posing As Impersonator
4. Liz Saves Di from Rapist
5. UFO Space Train Orbits Earth
6. Husband Admits: "I had PMS and Menopause"
7. Nun Abducted by Aliens in Search of Virgin Specimen
8. Six-Month-Old Baby Bends Spoon with Psychic Power
9. Mount Rushmore Presidents Crying Human Tears
10. Woman Boils Eggs by Holding Them in Her Hand
11. Ventriloquist Arrested for Fraud After He Uses Midgets for Dummies
12. UFO Aliens Pose As Surgeons and Implant Radios in Our Bodies
13. Widow Killed by Her Husband's Tombstone
14. Three-Foot Horn Grows Out of Man's Head
15. Missing Man Blown Away in Miami Hurricane Is Found in New Orleans

16. Lobster Boy's Wife Hired Hitman to Kill Him.
17. Turkey Farmer Attacked by His Birds on Thanksgiving Eve
18. Patient's Appendix Grows Back Four Times
19. Ouch! My Breasts Grew 52 Inches in Five Months
20. Man Swallows Hearing Aid and Gets Cramps When He's Around Loud Noises
21. Pop! Flying Champagne Cork Kills Bride
22. George Bush and Bill Clinton Brothers in Former Life
23. Man Superglues His Butt Shut
24. Busty Smuggler Stashes Drugs in Her Implants
25. Scientist Creates Mutant Vine and It Strangles Him

The sharp-eyed tabloid devotees will spot the only fake: #17. Skeptics and cynics, and readers of *The New Yorker*, will fare much worse.

STRANGE BEDFELLOWS

"Politicians are the same all over. They promise to build a bridge even where there is no river."

Nikita Khrushchev

Q: How do you know when politicians are lying?
A: They're talking.

When candidates for political office make promises and don't deliver, are they lying? Anyone with political savvy will say no. "No candidate can predict what will happen. They may have meant it when they said it and then circumstances changed." Any five-year-old will tell you, "They lied."

You know a politician is lying when:

▲ You know more about their spouse than their platform.
▲ They can prove their economic plans will work with a barrage of statistics but couldn't come up with their tax returns.
▲ They tell you they've had a vision.
▲ None of their promises call for higher taxes.
▲ They say they feel your pain but live in a mansion, drive in limos and graduated from Harvard.
▲ They ask you for your patience and understanding.
▲ Their family pet is more interesting than they are.

"An honest politician is one who when he is bought will stay bought."

SIMON CAMERON

"To my mind Judas Iscariot was nothing but a low, mean, premature congressman."

MARK TWAIN

"Politics is the gentle art of getting votes from the poor and campaign funds from the rich, by promising to protect each from the other."

OSCAR AMERINGER

"I once said cynically of a politician, 'He'll double cross that bridge when he comes to it.' "

OSCAR LEVANT

Two liars are company, three are a crowd, and four or more a chamber of commerce.

"There are three kinds of lies: lies, damned lies and statistics."

BENJAMIN DISRAELI

"I am different from Washington; I have a higher and grander standard of principle. Washington could not lie. I can lie, but I won't."

MARK TWAIN

Some people are liars; others merely tell the truth in such a way that nobody recognizes it.

"No public man can be just a little crooked."

HERBERT HOOVER

"I want you to stonewall it."

> RICHARD NIXON to staff on the news
> of the break-in at the Watergate
> headquarters of the Democratic party.
> Taped conversation, March 22, 1973.

"There will be no whitewash in the White House."

> RICHARD NIXON on the Watergate investigation.
> Press conference, April 17, 1973.

"People have got to know whether or not their president is a crook. Well I'm not a crook. I earned everything I got."

> RICHARD NIXON to the Associated Press
> managing editors. Disneyland,
> November 17, 1973.

"I want you to know . . . that I have no intention whatever of ever walking away from the job that the American people elected me to do for the people of the United States."

RICHARD NIXON

"When the president does it, it means it's not illegal."

RICHARD NIXON

"I never give them hell. I just tell them the truth and they think it's hell."

HARRY S.TRUMAN,
quoted in *Look*, April 3, 1956.

"I had a little knowledge. . . ."
"I've known what's going on there as a matter of fact, for quite a long time, a matter of years. It was my idea."

RONALD REAGAN, speaking on two separate
occasions about his knowledge
of Iran arms shipments.

"The rulers of the state are the only ones who should have the privilege of lying either at home or abroad; they may be allowed for the good of the state."

PLATO

TAX
EVASIONS

"It was as true," said Mrs. Barkis, . . . "as taxes is.
And nothing's truer than them."

Charles Dickens

The question isn't who lies on their taxes; the question is who doesn't. Mary Sprouse, author of *The Money Tax Handbook* and *If Time Is Money No Wonder I'm Not Rich*, has a unique perspective. As a tax attorney and a former IRS auditor, she has heard them all: "As far as the government is concerned, lying on your tax return is fraud. As a lawyer I feel compelled to tell you that. Here, however, are some of the things people have told me, and in parentheses my thoughts in reply."

I have no financial records because:

▲ I moved. (Just him, apparently, without his
belongings.)

▲ All my records were stolen. (On the day of the audit
he put all his financial records in a briefcase, which
was stolen when he left it in his car. This is a
national epidemic.)

▲ Gone with the wind. All my papers were blown away
when my friend's truck overturned. (This man kept
the most important papers he owned loose and not
even in a box?)

▲ They were lost in a fire. (When we said it would
have to be verified, we found out this taxpayer had
set the fire.)

▲ They're in a box. (No comment.)

THESE LIES ARE TRULY TAXING

"One man claimed his fish as a dependent. Since he couldn't give the age, he reported the fish's length."

A NEW YORK ACCOUNTANT

This and other fish stories are among our tax expert's favorites. The most frequent tax return boondoggles include:

▲ *Pets as exemptions.* This was so prevalent that when the federal government began to require social security numbers for all dependents over age one, the number of exemptions across the country dropped by more than 50 percent.

▲ *Offset gambling wins with gambling losses.* When someone makes a killing at the track, they can reduce the tax by providing verification of a similar loss. It appears that the lucky winners would collect losing tickets from the floor. This worked fine until we began to reject the losing stubs marked with footprints.

▲ *Charity donations*. Charities allow the donor to set the value of the item given. From the tax returns received, it would appear that people donate only unworn, designer clothing that has, unlike many investments, actually increased in value through the years.

▲ I *was robbed*. The cost of the goods or cash stolen can serve as an exemption. Is it a surprise that on the day that so many people's homes were robbed, they had an unusually large amount of cash in the house? Also, every piece of jewelry stolen was a gold family heirloom. No one owns costume anymore.

▲ *Business expenses*. Everyday items can be deducted if they are used solely for business. One man claimed the cost of his swimming pool, saying only his clients swam in it. Another claimed his Jaguar. He said he drove his secondhand car to his office parking lot, where he kept his Jag overnight. He then used the Jag only to drive to client appointments.

▲ *Employee salaries* are also a deductible expense. A popular ploy for businessmen is to put their children on the payroll, some at exceptionally high salaries for toddlers.

▲ *Loans to relatives*. In order to get a tax break on an unexpected gain, you may deduct an unpaid loan made in the same year. You wouldn't believe the number of people who write off bad debts to their relatives in the same year they cashed in.

▲ *Demonstration and promotional items*. Businessmen claim items they say they need to show off their products. How many VCRs do you need to sell a vacuum cleaner?

▲ *Home office*. You can deduct any space in your home whose sole purpose is for business use. Despite its popularity on tax returns, the kitchen table is not a "space."

LYING
IN
STYLE

The late actor David Niven found it hard to come to terms with the aging process and, in later life, still thought of himself as a young man. He recalled a visit to the London Boat Show with an attractive girl many years his junior. "Suddenly this hideous couple hove into view; a foul old creature with a crone of a wife. To my horror the man came over and introduced himself. 'Good heavens, Niven,' he said, 'I haven't seen you since you were at school.' When they'd gone I could sense that the girl was looking at me warily. 'Were you really at school with him?' she asked. 'Absolutely,' I told her. 'He was the music master.'"

From *The Little Brown Book of Anecdotes*, by Clifton Fadiman

HOW TO
BE A
LIE
DETECTOR

"The lady doth protest too much, methinks."

William Shakespeare, *Hamlet*

According to James Patterson and Peter Kim in their book *The Day America Told the Truth*, just about everyone lies. Ninety-one percent of us lie regularly. The majority of us find it hard to get through the week without lying. One in five can't make it through a single truthful day—and we're not talking about lapses of memory or slips of the tongue but about conscious, premeditated lies. And it's less likely that we refrain from lying because we think it's wrong. Not surprisingly, one of the most significant deterrents is fear of being caught.

So, given the facts, what are the real chances of getting caught? Among "professional" lie detectors, Paul Eckman and Maureen O'Sullivan reported in *American Psychologist*: "Only Secret Service [agents] performed better than chance and they were significantly more accurate than all other groups."

But there are certainly other professional lie detectors whose sharp instincts—and the all-too-common stupidity of the pernicious perjurers—make them human polygraphs:

▲ "In a family dispute you have to take the word of whoever's in the worst shape. My partner and I entered a house and found a man passed out on the floor with an imprint of an iron burned into his head. Despite what his wife claimed, he did not attack her. It turned out later that he'd been out partying and came home while she was ironing. She was so angry she hit him. Lucky she wasn't carving a turkey."

A NEW YORK CITY POLICE OFFICER

▲ "When someone uses the phrases 'Honestly' or 'To tell the truth' I can't help but wonder about what they've been telling me so far."

A CLINICAL PSYCHOLOGIST

▲ "People feel the need to have a certain number of sins. They come in with a list. 'I used the Lord's name in vain, cursed two times, had five impure thoughts.' It's like they're reading a list from the supermarket. It also makes me wonder what they're not telling me."

A ROMAN CATHOLIC PRIEST, QUEENS, NEW YORK

▲ "This kid we picked up confessed to a murder. We went to his house to notify his parents. When we got there, before I could say anything, his mother yells, 'My boy didn't kill that man. He was home with me. . . .' She went on to give details that only the murderer could know. So I said to her: 'Who said anything about a murder? For all you know we could be collecting for the Police Athletic League.'"

A NEW YORK CITY POLICE OFFICER

Ironically, in the business of catching a liar, machine is no better than man. In *The New England Journal of Medicine*, Dr. Robert Steinbrook said that any of the following factors could influence the outcome of the lie detector machines:

▲ the skills and experience of the test giver;
▲ the emotional state of the subject;
▲ the subject's prior experience with the test;
▲ the subject's perception of the test's validity.

Steinbrook also suggests the following countermeasures may be used by the subject prior to or during the exam to distort the results:

▲ minimize physical movement or the tensing of muscle groups;
▲ hypnosis;
▲ drugs;
▲ biofeedback.

"Experience teaches us that the man who looks you straight in the eye, particularly if he adds a firm handshake, is hiding something."

CLIFTON FADIMAN

The man who says he tells no lies is telling one.

"When a person cannot deceive himself, chances are against his being able to deceive other people."

MARK TWAIN

"The louder he talked of his honor, the faster we counted our spoons."

RALPH WALDO EMERSON

"There's one way to find out if a man is honest—ask him. If he says yes, you know he's crooked."

GROUCHO MARX

"There is nothing so pathetic as a forgetful liar."

F. M. KNOWLES

TEN TIPS TO LIE
LIKE A PRO

"Any fool can tell the truth, but it requires a man of
some sense to know how to lie well."

SAMUEL BUTLER

1. Visualize your lie so that it becomes a part of you and
   you become a part of it.
2. Don't skimp on detail. The more color you can give, the
   more real it sounds. Example: "The dog ate my home-
   work" isn't nearly as effective as "The Doberman attacked my loose leaf."
3. Never forget the important details of your story.
4. Use extremes. The more difficulty you say you've had to
   overcome the more sympathy you'll get.
5. Your lie should appear to benefit others as much as
   yourself.
6. Throw the bull with confidence. Learn to look people
   squarely in the eye. There's nothing better than an
   imposter with good posture.

7. If you're lying for a specific gain, don't make your agenda obvious.

8. Make the person you're lying to comfortable. A compliment comes in handy here. Tell them how much you trust them. When they return the feelings, you can lie to them with impunity.

9. Try gorilla-warfare lying: Camouflage your lies with statements or facts that the person already knows to be true.

10. Test the waters. Some people are more gullible than others. Why go after a hardhead when there may be a soft touch around?

THE GREAT LIE QUIZ!

Test your knowledge of lies and their synonyms. Each clue reflects a specific type of lie. For example: A Bridal Tale? Answer: A White Lie. How much do you know about lying?

1. Hen and cow, masculine?
2. Talk with split linguistics.
3. If The Donald exaggerated.
4. Nude, clock front tale.
5. Aquatic creature myth.
6. What a dentist might do.
7. King Midas' deception.
8. Cigarette box, hoaxes.
9. Rotate a thread.
10. Elasticizing the facts.

"The hardest tumble a man can make is to fall over his own bluff."

AMBROSE BIERCE

TALL TALES FROM THE BURLINGTON LIARS CLUB

If you enjoyed reading *Lies*, why not join The Burlington Liars Club? Vice President Don Reed told us that membership is open to all except lawyers and politicians. ''They're professional liars, we're just amateurs.'' Each year the club receives entries from all over the country and recently from China, Israel and France for its ''World Champion Liar's Contest.'' The following tall tales are reprinted with permission from *I Don't Lie and Other Lies from The Burlington Liars Club.*

"A man from Missouri said it was so cold there that he saw a politician standing on a corner with his hands in his own pockets."

"The apple tree that grows in the backyard bears a lot of fruit. Nice, big, juicy, red apples. One year I picked 250 bushels off that tree. Then I got a stepladder."

"It's so cold outside I saw a porcupine pull two needles from its back and knit itself a sweater."

"A friend of mine is so doggone lazy he married a pregnant woman."

"My sister is so thin she hula-hoops with a Cheerio."

"Our school district is so small that we had to teach drivers education and sex education in the same car."

"The fog in San Francisco is so thick the city council is considering putting the street signs in braille."

"The drought of '88 was so bad that the only water we could buy was dehydrated."

"The wind was so strong that one man's telephone wires stretched so far that when he called his neighbor across the street he was billed for long distance."

"The outback is so dry that one day when it did rain a man passed out and the only way to revive him was to throw a bucket of dust on him."

"I knew a man who was so dumb he couldn't empty a pail of water even if the directions were printed on the bottom."

"We raise a dozen cows on our farm. Last summer it was so hot and dry that the cows gave powdered milk."

"How cold was it one day last winter? I dunno but when I went outside my fever blister turned into a cold sore."

"It was sooo cold the other day in my hometown that as I was walking to work I looked over my shoulder to see my shadow going back into the house for a warmer coat."

"It was so windy in Seymor, we had to rename the dog. Spot went outside. Now we call him Whitey."

"I caught a large fish in northern Wisconsin last summer. There was no scale around to weigh it, but the picture we took weighed 28 pounds."

"There is a lake in northern Wisconsin that is so small even the fish are curved."

"My father doesn't use bait or tackle when he fishes. He feeds chewing tobacco to the fish and hits them over the head when they come up to spit."

"We have a house in our town that is so old the only thing that keeps it from falling is the termites holding hands."

"Our neighbor's dog is so ugly it has to sneak up on its water dish to get a drink."

"At my school the hamburgers are so tough they formed a gang and stole a car."

The Burlington Liars Club accepts entries for its contest year-round. Even if you don't enter, you can become a member by sending a dollar to cover the cost of the membership card. Mail to:

Don Reed
The Burlington Liars Club
149 North Oakland Ave.
Burlington, Wisconsin 53105

For information about a copy of the club's publication, write to:

Shepherd Inc.
1110 Bluff Street
Dubuque, Iowa 52001
Re: *I Don't Lie and Other Lies from The Burlington Liars Club.*

"All men are born truthful and die liars."

VAUVENARGUES